I Wonder...
Did Jesus Have a Pet Lamb?

Janette Oke

ILLUSTRATED BY
CORBERT GAUTHIER

BETHANY
BACKYARD®
MINNEAPOLIS, MN 55438

The Bible tells us about Jesus' birth. He was born in Bethlehem, and his mother, Mary, bundled him up and tucked him into a manger for his bed. An angel told shepherds where he was, and they came to look at him. There he was—a tiny newborn baby snuggled into the hay. We think about his story every year at Christmastime when we celebrate his birthday.

The Bible has lots and lots of stories about when Jesus was a man. He called people to follow him. He visited many villages, telling wonderful stories and making blind men see and lame men walk again. He even fed a whole bunch of people with just one little boy's lunch! And another time, when a father and mother were very sad and crying because their little girl had died, Jesus took her hand and made her well again. He loved children and taught that everyone who wanted to go to Heaven should be trusting and loving like a child.

Yes, the Bible tells us Jesus was a very special baby—and a very special man.

But do you ever wonder about Jesus after he was a baby, before he became a man? I wonder what he was like when he was just a boy.

Did the boy Jesus have favorite things he liked to do? When he was done helping Joseph in the carpenter shop, did he like to play? He didn't have a scooter or a bicycle or a skateboard because those things weren't around when Jesus was a boy. So what did he do for fun?

Did he like to go fishing in the Sea of Galilee with his grandpa?

Did he sit on the bank or in a boat and wiggle his toes in the cool water while he waited for a pull on his fishing line?

I wonder. . . .

I wonder what his toys were like. There weren't trains or trucks or Legos or robots. Maybe his dad carved him a donkey from leftover olive wood. Maybe the little wooden donkey even pulled a wagon. Or maybe Jesus built things himself with pieces of wood left over from his dad's carpenter shop. Did he make little houses or mangers or even a miniature temple?

I wonder....

I wonder if Jesus had a pet. If he did, was it a small, woolly lamb or a long-eared baby donkey? Maybe it was a bird in a wicker cage—or a turtle he kept in an earthenware jar. Or maybe he had a silky-haired cat that liked to curl up on his bed, or a puppy that liked to romp and play.

I wonder....

I wonder if Jesus liked to go to his grandma's house. Did she put her hand on his head and look at him with love and pride in her eyes as she told him he was getting s-o-o-o big he would soon catch up to her? And was she pleased and proud when he brought her a handmade box he had made to hold her market coins?

Or small shells he had gathered beside the sea?

I wonder....

I wonder what he liked to eat. Not ice cream—there was no ice in a freezer to keep it cold back in those days. Not wiggly Jell-O—it hadn't been invented yet. Jesus and his family didn't have hot dogs or potato chips or spaghetti or pizza, either. Did he like bread and fish?

Did he ever climb a tree to pick a ripe, juicy peach?

Did his mommy ever make him puddings

or cakes with honey drizzled over

them to make them taste good?

I wonder....

I wonder where Jesus went to school. They didn't have big buildings or classrooms with round globes or art-project displays or chalkboards, but they might have had slates to write on. They sure didn't have computers! But Jesus must have had good teachers, and he must have been a good student—when he was only twelve years old, he went to the temple, where the smartest people were, and he asked good questions and gave good answers when the grown-ups asked him things.

How did he learn so much?

I wonder....

There are so many things I wonder! Did his mommy save his very first tooth or a dark curl of his baby hair? Were his wool clothes sometimes itchy and too warm? Did he have chores to do each day? I wonder if Jesus liked music and if he learned to play a tune on a reed pipe or strum on a lute. Did he ever fall and scratch his knees or elbows and have his mommy kiss the hurt and wipe away the tears and send him back out to play?

I wonder....

I wonder if Jesus had a best friend. Did he fit in with the other boys in Nazareth, or did some of them think he was different and call him names or even push him around? If they did, was it hard for him not to get mad and be mean back? Did he say a quick prayer to his heavenly Father to help him do what was right? Did he sometimes feel lonesome for his home in Heaven with all its wonderfully familiar and safe things?

I wonder....

He must have been very special as a boy. If I had lived a long time ago when Jesus lived in Palestine, I would have wanted to be his friend. But you know what? I can be his friend. Even now. Jesus says, "You are my friends if you obey me." I want to obey Jesus and be his friend. And that is the most wonderful thing of all to think about!

God sets the lonely in families. Psalm 68:6

How blessed we are to have two new Russian children join our family.
Marvin and Laurel Logan have added Vladimir (Adam) and Anastasia (Anna) to their four.
Nate, Jessica, Jackie, and Alex are welcoming these two young siblings with love and joy.

And God has also blessed us with the August 1, 2004, arrival of Wesley Frederick,
a brother for Brian and son of Lavon and Monica.

To these three precious grandkids I lovingly dedicate *I Wonder*.
May you early in life discover the wonder of who Jesus is.

❧

I Wonder...Did Jesus Have a Pet Lamb?
Text © 2004 by Janette Oke
Illustrations © 2004 by Corbert Gauthier

Published by Bethany House Publishers
11400 Hampshire Avenue South
Bloomington, Minnesota 55438
www.bethanyhouse.com

Bethany House Publishers is a Division of
Baker Book House Company, Grand Rapids, Michigan.

Printed in China.

Library of Congress Cataloging-in-Publication data applied for.

ISBN 0-7642-2901-X